COMPACT
CYMRU

CW00501874

Snowdonia Slate 2
The story with photographs
Des Marshall

Gwasg Carreg Gwalch

First published in 2022
© text & photos: Des Marshall

All rights reserved. No part of this publication
may be reproduced, stored in a retrieval system,
or transmitted in any form or by any means,
electronic, electrostatic, magnetic tape, mechanical,
photocopying, recording, or otherwise, without prior
permission of the authors of the works herein.

ISBN: 978-1-84524-397-5
Cover design: Eleri Owen

Published by Gwasg Carreg Gwalch,
12 Iard yr Orsaf, Llanrwst, Wales LL26 0EH
tel: 01492 642031
email: books@carreg-gwalch.cymru
website: www.carreg-gwalch.cymru

Hazards and Problems
Take Notice, Take Care

The author and the publishers stress that walkers should be aware of the dangers that may occur on all walks.

– check local weather forecast before walking; do not walk up into mist or low clouds
– use local OS maps side by side with walking guides
– wear walking boots and appropriate clothing
– do not take any unnecessary risks – conditions can change suddenly and can vary from season to season
– take special care when accompanied by children or dogs
– when walking on roads, ensure that you are conspicuous to traffic from either direction

Page 1: Random slate stacked against the incline wall at Bryn Hafod y Wern; Left: A tramway bridge at Braich quarry

Introduction

This second book of *Snowdonia Slate – The story with photographs*, compliments and adds to the descriptions of the first. It is written in a different format to book 1 in that the sites are described alphabetically. The quarries and mines featured, although not as well known or familiar, are of as much importance and influence for the areas they are situated. Just like the first book this one tries to illustrate and record the current surface remains of these other abandoned slate mines and quarries of Snowdonia. I have done this to increase awareness of these important places and photograph what remains for future generations before what can be seen today disintegrates further at the hands of nature or vandals.

This book too does not pretend to be definitive as there are well over 500 mines and quarries, including trials, in Snowdonia. Slate quarrying and mining is all part of Snowdonia's heritage and played an important part in the development of the towns and villages and brought prosperity to many of these. I must re-iterate here that I feel the slate industry of yesteryear needs conserving and photographic records taken. The slate industry in Wales has been dubbed '*the most 'Welshest' of industries*'. Small scale quarrying continues to this day in a few quarries.

Herein, just as in book 1 the remains of what once was are impressive. Apart from the huge amount of spoil there are the remains of buildings, such as barracks and waliau; drum houses; tramways; railway lines and of course remarkable inclines. Fortunately still, many of the remains are indeed quite substantial. Of course there are some very impressive deep pits that somehow are not too obtrusive. Although the huge scar of Dinorwig on Elidir Fawr is stark, it is gazed upon in wonder as to how much of the mountainside has been removed Many of the mines and quarries are situated on the edge of the Park but are intertwined and integral to the history of it.

Oddly, the two major quarries of the area Dinorwig and Penrhyn are outside the Park. I feel that as they played an important part in the history of the area they should be included. Towns grew as the industry grew, for example Llanberis, Bethesda, Blaenau Ffestiniog and even larger ones such as Porthmadog, Bangor and Caernarfon, they all depended on the slate industry to some degree.

Sadly with the demise of the industry some of these towns are mere shadows of their former glory. Run down and forlorn Bethesda for instance is one. Llanberis is rising Phoenix like being close to major attractions. Although outside the Park, Blaenau Ffestiniog is reinventing itself as the adventure capital of Snowdonia. Other towns and villages connected to the industry are sadly neglected but the spirit of the people lives on. The main reason for writing book 1 and now this second one is because I feel strongly about conserving what is left is. Nowadays much of the history of these places has now been relegated to the past and forgotten about with little or no thought or regard about preserving or even conserving any of what does remain. That is a very sad reflection of the toil and hardship the quarrymen and miners experienced whilst putting their lives at risk to obtain slate. Tourism in the area is the modern day equivalent to the slate industry.

This book is not a walking guide. There are books that do describe walks and trails to many of the quarries and mines. *The Snowdonia Slate Trail* is an 85 miles long walk around the major quarrying and mining areas of northern Snowdonia. It is superbly described in the guide by Aled Owen. Another book describes day walks to many of the mines and quarries in Snowdonia and is titled *Exploring*

Snowdonia's Slate Heritage written by me. Another, also by me, *Day walks from the Slate Trail* is a guide describing day walks from the actual 'Slate Trail' itself to give a greater and fuller understanding of the slate industry. These walks follow paths and tracks on public rights of way and do not venture underground. If you feel tempted to look at these remains be mindful that some of these quarries and mines are situated in bleak surroundings high up on a mountainside. Keep well away from quarry edges as they are loose and can collapse unpredictably. It is important to have the right clothing and footwear for the conditions prevailing. Take note of the recommendations in the guidebooks.

I have given map references to the quarries and mines but please bear in mind that they are very dangerous places. It is definitely most unwise to venture underground without an experienced and qualified guide. There are many areas of loose rock on the walls and floors along with dangerous ceilings. Mines used for commercial exploration are checked by mining engineers who give a report on their suitability of this activity for the various companies that specialise in underground trips. It is NOT recommended to venture on to the spoil heaps. They are loose and can be very slippery especially in the wet when a layer of lichen acts like soap. Please be aware that slate is also extremely sharp and can cause nasty cuts and lacerations. If you want to experience more things slate I have included a list of other attractions at the back of the book. This includes companies that undertake specialist mining trips with fully qualified leaders for those wanting to learn more about the internal workings of a mine. Not only are they qualified the leaders have a great deal of experience and knowledge about mining history.

Some of the pictures were taken with permission from farmers or landowners. As such these features are found on private land. Where this is the case I have indicated so. The best and most useful maps to use are the 1:25,000 Ordnance Survey Outdoor Leisure series. These are: OL17 Snowdon/Yr Wyddfa; OL18 Harlech, Porthmadog &Bala/Y Bala, OL 23 Cadair Idris & Llyn Tegid and Explorer 254 Lleyn Peninsula East/Pen Llŷn Ardal Ddwyreiniol.

Under the leadership of Gwynedd County Council the UNESCO World Heritage nomination was put together with key partners. The proposal took into consideration the variety of technology, organisation, social and environmental impacts of the slate industry in the mountain landscapes on North Wales which once dominated world production. UNESCO approval for the six slate areas was approved on the 28th July 2021. The areas are – Penrhyn, Dinorwig, Nantlle Valley, Gorseddau and Prince of Wales (as one area), Ffestiniog and Bryneglwys.

The key aims of the nomination were:

1. Heritage led regeneration
2. Conservation
3. Economic development
4. Community and skills development
5. Re-connecting communities with heritage
6. Promote and celebrate the important global role of the Welsh slate industry
7. Unified story

Finally, I recommend a visit to the National Slate Museum to appreciate the plethora of quarrying and mining artefacts exhibited there as well as being able to watch a demonstration on how roofing slates are split from blocks of slate in one of the workshops. Certainly a good bet on a wet day.

For amusement a list of common slate sizes are listed below as well as a few other facts and figures. It will be noted that the names of the different sizes are predominantly 'female'. Sizes are in inches.

Empress 26 x 16
Princess 24 x 14
Duchess 24 x 12
Small Duchess 22 x 12
Marchioness 22 x 11
Broad Countess 20 x 12
Countess 20 x 10
Small Countess 18 x 10
Viscountess 18 x 9
Wide Lady 16 x 10
Broad Lady 16 x 9
Lady 16 x 8
Small Lady 14 x 8
Narrow Lady 14 x 7
Double 12 x 6
Single 10 x 5

Many other sizes and names existed with over 30 being known at the end of the 19th century. 'Queens' could have been anything from 30 x 18 to 36 x 26 or even larger. 'Princesses' were often termed 'Fourteens'. 'Putts' were 14 x 12 sometimes called 'Headers' and 'Ladies Putts' were 13 x 10, 'Damp Course' slates came in many sizes from 20 x 9 down to 9 x 4½.

In 1872 a Countess slate cost a halfpenny in old pre-decimal currency and 135 years later the same aize slate cost £3.

North Wales' slate is the best in the world. Apart from being very durable it is strong, light and, of course, waterproof.

The output of roofing slate from Gwynedd slate quarries was enough to roof 14 million terraced houses.

The longest industrial dispute in British industrial history was at Penrhyn Quarry just outside Bethesda which lasted for three years starting on the 22nd November 1900. Unfortunately it heralded the demise of the reliability of slate production and orders fell sharply with thousands of workers laid off.

Slate was exported worldwide but some of the major recipients were the Channel Islands with 580, 000 tons; Belgium 431,000; Argentina 404,000; British Africa 290,000; West Indies 114,000; Germany 41,000; Australia 5,500 and Denmark 3,500.

What is Slate? Its Formation and Uses

Slate is a metamorphic rock. This means it has been altered from its original sedimentary composition. The word slate stems from the old English *slat* or perhaps even *sclat* and the French word meaning 'to split', *escalater*. The formation of slate in Snowdonia began around 500 million years ago, or Cambrian period for the Dinorwig, Penrhyn and Nantlle areas and around 450 million years ago, or Ordovician period, for Abergynolwyn, Aberllefenni, Corris and Ffestiniog slate. Originally depositions of fine sediments of clay minerals flaky in character formed a mudstone. Minerals in this determined the colour the slate was eventually to become. Depositions continued over several million years and huge pressures turned the mudstone into shale.

Continued pressure and great heat caused a chemical change to occur. The original clay minerals broke down to become other minerals such as mica and feldspar, the main constituents of this reformed and different rock, slate. Interestingly the minerals had reformed at an angle to the bedding planes. This was the line of cleavage. Some mines, notably in Gaewern a part of the Braich Goch mine complex above Corris have pure white calcite formations such as curtains, stalactites and stalagmites normally only seen in caves.

The slate above Bethesda and Nantlle tends to have a reddish purple tinge to it, whilst around Blaenau Ffestiniog and Corris it is blue grey and is much finer grained. Generally it is slate from the Cambrian period that provides the most durable and hardest slate. In fact roofing slate from the quarries in Snowdonia were regarded as the finest and most durable in the whole world withstanding the effects of extreme weather, was unaffected by frost and totally impervious to water. Combined with the cheap cost of production until the 1930's, slate was the most popular roofing material.

The Blaenau Ffestiniog vein was called the Old Vein and provided excellent roofing slate whist the Corris was named the Narrow Vein and provided excellent slab. Another slate, found outside of Snowdonia and this guide, was formed in the Silurian period, around 430 million years ago. This is the least durable of the types but it provided good slab for indoor use.

Nowadays slate is used for a plethora of tourist souvenirs but in the past there have been many other uses. The best snooker tables had slate beds. Apart from roofing slate other uses included building material, walling, slate plank fencing, flooring, sills, lintels, quoins. It was used to form vats in both the chemical and brewing industries on account of its impervious nature. Cisterns, sold as 'flat packs', were manufactured. In farming it was used in pig sties and cowsheds, dairies and larders not to mention the Victorian 'privy' or Gents toilets. It was also used for making coffins, some of which were re-usable (probably for pauper burials) and gravestones. Slate was also used in the electricity trade where it was used for switchboards and insulation. Interestingly slate is also used in the fashion industry for making lipstick and the production of soap.

Methods of Extracting Slate

Slate is extracted by one of three methods. The first is '*Hillside Working*'. Here it is either face working where the slate is dug into the hillside to form a single level. If the slate is of good quality and appears to be a continuous large vein it often becomes a quarry and is then extracted from multiple galleries or terraces. The second method is '*Pit Working*'. Here a slate vein is followed down with adits or levels being driven to make life easier for transportation of the raw product. Finally there is '*Underground Working*'. This occurs when there would be too much surface material to be removed. The vein is accessed by driving adits or levels. Work would then commence along the top of the vein by driving what is known as a roofing shaft. From this progress would then be downward and across to form a chamber. A typical size would be around 22 metres wide. Another chamber would then be started leaving an intervening pillar some 13 metres wide that would act as a support for the roof. Many chambers could be developed in any mine by this process.

With today's modern mining techniques a method called '*un-topping*' is used to remove the surface of the ground above the vein and rob the pillars as these would be good quality slate. In its most simple form slate was extracted by attacking the slate exposure by basic and simple means such as levering and cutting out usable blocks. The tools used for this were a big oak mallet called, in Welsh a '*Rhys*' and '*Plug and Feathers*'. These were wedges that expanded the rock when driven into cracks.

As these workings expanded it became evident that more rock was needed so blasting took place. Initially this was black powder. Prior to mechanisation a shot hole was drilled by the use of a '*Jumpah*', a long weighted iron rod. This was a very laborious slow method. After 1880 or so compressed air drills were used, much quicker but incredibly noisy. Eventually high explosives were used but this tended to shatter the rock. Only 10% of the rock extracted was usable. The usable blocks going to be used for roofing slates were then split using a chisel to a suitable thickness before being dressed to the required size. They were then held over a fixed blade, the '*Celfi*' and trimmed by the use of a tool similar to a knife, '*Cyllell*'.

Further developments took place with the advent of water power in the early 19th century. Circular saws developed and in the mid-20th century diamond circular saws came into use and are now universal. They are huge things having blades two metres in diameter and even slightly larger. Instead of the coarse cut of the water powered saws these saws have a very fine cut but used water for cooling the blade. Having seen these work it is absolutely amazing to see a three ton block of slate over 300mm thick and 1.5 metres long sliced just as a knife goes through butter. Mechanical dressing developed around the same time as circular saws and was operated by hand or foot. However, splitting the slate still remains a manual process. Many attempts to mechanise this process failed.

Bangor
Conwy
A470
4 Bethesda
Caernarfon
Llanrwst
A4086
A408 9
6 11
A5
22 2
Llanberis
Betws-y-coed
3
10
19
21
A487
13
7
18 17
A498
15
Beddgelert
A5
14
Porthmadog
Blaenau
16 Ffestiniog
A4212
SNOWDONIA
Y Bala
A470
A494
Harlech
Afon
A496
Mawddach
Bermo
(Barmouth)
Dolgellau
5 20
A487 1
12
8 Afon
A493
Dyfi
A470
A489
Tywyn
Machynlleth
Aberdyfi

The Sites

Abercorris

Map: Ordnance Survey 1:25,000
Explorer OL 23 Cadair Idris & Llyn Tegid
Grid reference: SH 754 089

Abercorris quarry is known locally as Cwmodyn and on a band of slate called the 'Narrow Vein'. The slate from this is of much higher quality than the 'Broad Vein'. Quarrying operations commenced here about 1863 but production fluctuated greatly over the years due to several financial misfortunes of the various companies that took over and going from boom to bust. Peaking in 1902 at 1,132 tons from a maximum of 45 workers the quarry closed in 1914. It re-opened in 1920 and sporadic working continued until the 1950's although with a considerable drop in the number of men. Very limited quarrying continued, but with limited power, working was restricted from 16.00 to midnight! The quarry had two workings on the hillside that developed into pits. These were accessed by tunnels. Some later workings were underground. An incline took the quarried material initially to a water powered mill some 122 metres, 400 feet below whilst the later mill was electrically powered. Today, considerable high quality slate remains.

Sadly this site is very overgrown and little is visible without jungle bashing. However, the lovely and excellent Corris Heritage walk passes a charming Renaissance Italian garden on the way. A short distance up the track, beyond the garden, is a fine caban or canteen below the quarry itself. The walk then enters woodland sporting more ruins. Cabans were where the quarry workers met to have lunch, to rest and discuss life in general. The mill itself was to the left of the caban.

1. *The Caban below the workings;*
2. *Ruins lurking in the dense wood*

Corris was once a very thriving community. At the turn of the 19th century there were 14 shops, 4 chapels and a church, 3 banks, 2 schools, 2 pubs, had its own bakery, a weekly newspaper and had a prize winning silver band not to mention successful football, cricket and rugby teams.

The walk from Corris passes a cottage that dates to 1841. The 'Renaissance Italian' garden to its left started being built in 1980. Included are the 'Leaning Tower of Pisa' the 'Rialto Bridge' in Venice, 'Palladio' the most imitated architect in history is well represented. There is no access but most of the miniature replicas can be seen from the track. Of great note here though is a plaque to Wilfred Owen M.C. He was born on the 18th March 1893 and died in battle during the 1st World War on 4th November 1918 only a week before the Armistice was signed! Wilfred is regarded as one of the most eminent poets of that war. His poetry vividly portrayed the horrors of war. A few lines etched onto a slab of slate reads –

The pallor of girls' brows shall be their pall;
Their flowers the tenderness of patient minds,
And each slow dusk a drawing down of blinds.

These are the last 3 lines from, perhaps, his most poignant poem *'Anthem for Doomed Youth'*.

1. View over Corris; 2. Part of the Italianate Garden

Alexandra

Map: Ordnance Survey 1:25,000
Explorer OL 17 Snowdon/Yr Wyddfa
Grid reference: SH 519 562

Also known as Cors y Bryniau. Opened in 1860, this became a three pit quarry. Nowadays pits one and two are merged whilst pit three is buried. Moel Tryfan quarry merged with Alexandra in the 1960's. At its peak Alexandra produced 6,000 tons per annum and employed over 200 men. The finished product was sent along a spectacular two miles long 'Alpine' tramway to the head of the Bryngwyn incline. There were three steam powered mills along with an extensive internal locomotive powered tramway system. The mills closed in the late 1930's. Some small scale work continues at Moel Tryfan.

Little remains of this once large site. The outline of the flattened mill can be traced, along with the ruined

Ruins above Alexandra looking to Moel Eilio

once impressive electricity sub-station. Other ruins comprise the office, workshops and weigh bridge.

The walk from Y Fron is a delightful one passing firstly Braich Quarry it reaches Alexandra. The view of Snowdon is very fine and of course the Nantlle Ridge. Continuing a short distance along the 'Alpine' tramway track-bed a faint path branches left to

The ruins above the quarry pit with part of the Nantlle Ridge forming the skyline. Left to right are Mynydd Drws y Coed and Trum y Ddysgl.

the summit of Moel Tryfan 427 metres, 1,401 feet, a geologically interesting place. The summit rocks were deposited during the Ice Age 20 to 30,000 years ago because the glacial Irish Sea was in conflict with ice on the Welsh mainland. Sand and gravel from the sea along with shells and wood were dredged from the seabed by the marine ice and thrust southwards to be deposited on the summit of Moel Tryfan. Today the summit still plays and important part in the development of glacial theories and Pleistocene studies.

There is an outstanding panoramic view from the summit and takes in Snowdon 1,085 metres, Mynydd Mawr 698 metres 2,290 feet, all of the Nantlle Ridge, Yr Eifl on the Llŷn Peninsula, Anglesey, Caernarfon and Moel Eilio 726 metres, 2,382 feet.

1. Looking towards Moel Eilio with the ruins above the quarry pit; 2. The mill area of Alexandra and the start of the 'Alpine' railway

1. *Looking to the summit of Moel Tryfan;*
2. *Snowdon from Alexandra*

Braich

*Map: Ordnance Survey 1:25,000
Explorer OL 17 Snowdon/Yr Wyddfa.
Grid reference: SH 510 552*

Braich incorporates Braich Melyn, New Reach and Bwlch y Llyn. There are few remains here. Most notable is the flooded pit. Above it there are vestiges of *waliau* and other buildings associated with the quarry. The impressive views across to the Nantlle Ridge are memorable. The quarry was worked from the early 19th century and then in 1868, when a steam powered mill was built, development increased greatly. Output in 1882 was 2,614 tons gleaned from the workforce of 124. Closure came in 1911.

Originally slate was transported with difficulty and it was not until 1868 that it was able to connect to the Nantlle Railway. When the Bryngwyn branch of the North Wales Narrow

Building remains on top of the quarry looking to Moel Tryfan in the distance

Remains at the top of the quarry

Gauge Railway (NWNGR) reached the quarry development increased rapidly. The 610mm, 2 feet gauge line ran from Dinas (now on the Welsh Highland Railway) close to Caernarfon. Caernarfon was connected to the main line as well as being a port for the shipment of slate.

Access is possible by following a track up from Y Fron to a very pleasant path that wanders up and above the right hand side of the flooded pit. The ruins over to the left are easily reached from this path.

The flooded quarry pit

Bryn Hafod y Wern

Map: Ordnance Survey 1:25,000
Explorer OL 17 Snowdon/Yr Wyddfa
Grid reference: SH 631 693

Also known as Royal Bangor. The flooded pit is downhill of the mill area. As such all the quarried material had to be up-hauled due to the unavailability of land below. Quarrying commenced around 1780 by the Pennants of Penrhyn but abandoned by them in 1845. It was re-opened the same year by The Royal Bangor Slate Company. They then built the mills but ceased work in 1884 when the Pennants severed their water supply.

The pit was 61 metres, 200 feet deep but today it is flooded. Slate and rubbish was raised to a landing platform by a water powered incline. Good slate was lowered from the landing platform by a short self acting incline to a small mill then down

again to another mill. The mill wheels were driven in tandem by water from these haulages. The finished product was carted to Bangor. Before closure output in 1882 was 2,198 tons per annum from about 65 men possibly half the number of the previous decade!

1. The archway below the tramway;
2. An incline wall; 3. Launder pillars;
4. The flooded quarry pit

There is still quite a lot to see at this accessible site. The highlight is a fine pointed arch which gives access to the upper mills area. Beyond are launder pillars. Bryn Hall was the owner's house. It is still lived in today and has a wonderful arched entrance gate.

Cambergi

Map: Ordnance Survey 1:25,000
Explorer OL 23 Cadair Idris & Llyn Tegid
Grid reference: SH 765 108

Also known as Wenallt. Slate produced was from the Broad Vein so was predominantly slab. Visually from the road the site is difficult to interpret. An incline leading down to the mill is now obscured. This serviced 9 working levels above it. A tenth level was at the head of the incline. At its base on the valley floor was the mill dating from 1873 built by the Cambergi Slate Quarry Company, the owners, who were mostly from Pontypool. One of them, D. Williams, may well have been David Williams who was at that time a director of the Pontypool Iron and Tin Plate Co. Ltd.

Money quickly ran out and in 1875 the lease was surrendered. The land had been leased to them by the Anwyl family. Very soon after, a new lease for

Looking up the steep hillside to the workings

39 years, was taken up by Sarah Griffiths and her daughter Elizabeth at £10 per annum. Another family member, the brother of Elizabeth, Griffith William Griffiths joined them. He had worked at FRON

FRAITH SH 759 125 and SH 757 121 further up the valley with very little success. Also, he had fallen out with his partner John Hughes Jones so was probably very pleased with getting to grips with Cambergi. Product was carted down to Aberllefenni for transportation by the Corris Railway.

In 1877 Cambergi slate did not match the quality of its equipment so Griffith started digging on the other side of the valley at HENGAE SH 759 115. In 1883, short of funds, he wanted to either mortgage or even sell Cambergi. He was unable to do either but did get a loan and was selling roofing slate in 1886. Shortly after he closed the working down and sold off some of his machinery. Life between the siblings became acrimonious, mainly due to finance. Many minor debts were piling up but each one did get paid but it took until 1920 to do

1. *Remains of Cambergi Mill;*
2. *Slate slab fencing*

so! Small time work continued through the years but it is obvious from the lack of waste that not much slate was ever produced.

The mill is now seriously degraded. An aqueduct supplied water to a breast shot 9.14 metres, 30 feet waterwheel. An inventory taken in 1883 ten years after the original quarry company, the Cambergi Slate Quarry Company, indicated that the mill had nine Owen sawing machines, a planer, a saw sharpener, a grinding stone and ten India Rubber belts!

Nearby are the 'Blue Cottages' built for the Aberllefenni quarry workers. These are now re-built but originally had slate fenced allotments and a pair of outside lavatories that were used by the whole row some distance in front.

1. View of the Cambergi Mill area;
2. Ruins in a field below the incline;
3. Roadside ruins below the incline

Cefn Du

Map: Ordnance Survey 1:25,000
Explorer OL 17 Snowdon/Yr Wyddfa
Grid reference: SH 566 603

Also known as Chwarel Hir it incorporated Chwarel Fawr and the older workings of Chwarel Huw Dafydd, Chwarel Morgan, Chwarel Owen, Chwarel y Maen and Chwarel y Pigia. Although just outside the National Park boundary they can be accessed from Llanberis via Bwlch y Groes or much more easily from Waunfawr by following an increasingly rough road to a large car parking area where the tarmac ends. The workins opened in the 18th century or possibly even earlier. It was part of the Cilgwyn & Cefn Du Company 1800. It was a pit quarry but had locomotive tramways on two levels. Amalgamating with Cambrian Quarry SH 566 603 and the Llanberis Slate Company in 1878 it produced 5,640 tons from a workforce of 197 in 1882. In 1879 it was reported that there were 4 steam engines, 2 waterwheels and a water turbine on site. Later on it produced its own electricity. Closure came around 1928.

Associated with Cefn Du is the nearby and impressive crater of CHWAREL FAWR SH 552 600. Like Cefn Du it is of 18th century vintage or perhaps, even earlier. It's name suggests it was a large undertaking but until the late 1860's it was very small. Its product was originally carted to Caernarfon via Waunfawr.

The huge jagged pit of Cefn Du

View into Chwarel Fawr looking towards Moel Eilio

Looking down into Chwarel Fawr

Foel

Map: Ordnance Survey 1:25,000
Explorer OL 17 Snowdon/Yr Wyddfa.
Grid reference: SH 717 556

Incorporating Bryn Cyple, Moel Siabod and Trewydir workings. Foel commenced life around 1835 and developed as a pit. It was worked on five levels with two of them having tunnel access to the pit. There were two mills on site. The highest one possibly had a sand saw powered by a waterwheel whilst the lower, which possibly took its place, was driven by a turbine or Pelton wheel driving the saws. Slate was sent down via an incline to a tramway and then by further inclines to a mill at Pont Cyfyng. This mill, too, used sand saws. Annual tonnage was not high with under a dozen men producing a maximum of about 500. The site was intermittently worked until closure in 1884. The Foel inclines were then

Ruined buildings at Foel

rented out to Rhos Quarry.

There are many ruins including the remains of three *waliau*, with cantilevered slate roofs, where the slate was dressed into roofing slates. It is a ruinous landscape but the

Ruins below the flooded quarry pit

The flooded quarry pit

remains of the barracks are very impressive making it well worth the visit.

There is a clear path from Pont Cyfyng to Foel, part of one of the walking routes up Moel Siabod 872 metres, 2,861 feet. The quarry is situated at an altitude of 470 metres, 1,542 feet. As such the weather can be unpredictable so if venturing here please dress accordingly. There is car parking at Bryn Glo close to Pont Cyfyng and a lay-by at the opposite side of the road to the car park.

1. Ruins and small internal incline;
2. Looking down on the ruined waliau;
3. Ruined buildings

Gaewern

*Map: Ordnance Survey 1:25,000
Explorer OL 23 Cadair Idris & Llyn Tegid
Grid reference: SH 745 086*

Also known as Tal-y-llyn and incorporates Glanderi, Rhognant and Sgwd. Slate mined here came from the 'Narrow Vein'. Along with Braich Goch Gaewern dominated the mining activity in the area. The older workings to the west were known as Sgwd whilst the eastern ones were called Rhognant. The open workings close to the road were the early workings of Glanderi. These 'trials', 'diggings' or 'scratchings' started before the 18th century. Early speculators had their hopes dashed until Gaewern was taken over by BRAICH GOCH SH 748 079 in or around 1830. Much of the extraction took place underground where huge chambers were created. In 1832 slate was sand sawn but later replaced by

Looking across to Gaewern from above Upper Corris

hand cranked circular saws. Gaewern was worked in conjunction with. Part of this complex system is home to King Arthur's Labyrinth a show mine experience especially suited to the young. The more adventurous can explore the real workings on a number of tailored trips undertaken

and led by Corris Mine Explorers.

Currently there is no access. When access was possible and exploration feasible the impressive entrance

1. Looking up an incline to the ruined drumhouse; 2. Crude steps rising through a spoil heap

followed levels into and out of chambers. One level ended at some very fine stained iron rock whilst another had some impressive pure white calcite formations. After descending through the mine the exit was onto an old tramway. When access is once again possible it is well worth a visit to this very complicated site.

1. The ruined drum-house; 2. The mine workings as seen from Abercorris Mine. Note the drum-house on the far right

Garreg Fawr

Map: Ordnance Survey 1:25,000
Explorer OL 17 Snowdon/Yr Wyddfa
Grid reference: SH 538 582

This was a very small working but a visit is recommended to view the fanciful castellated squat tower like building. This was, perhaps, an office for the quarry that dates back to the early 1800's. Later, underground development took place. Work was undertaken sporadically until the mid 1880's. In 1883 for example 96 tons were produced from 6 men. Occasional work continued until the 1960's. Originally output was carted to Caernarfon. There are a few other remains such as dressing sheds and a more modern brick building that housed an air compressor.

Interestingly the unique ex Hafod y Llan three speed saw table developed by John Owen of Bangor used here for many years has been restored and can be seen at the National Slate Museum in Llanberis.

View of the fanciful castellated tower

Glanrafon

Map: Ordnance Survey 1:25,000 Explorer OL 17 Snowdon/Yr Wyddfa.
Grid reference: SH 581 540

Also known as West Snowdon, Glanrafon was the last quarry to open in the area and also the last successful one to be opened in Wales. Operating on a small scale, until 1878, Glanrafon developed very quickly with the arrival of the North Wales Narrow Gauge Railway (NWNGR). In 1882 production was at its highest with 1,725 tons produced by 92 men. By the mid 1890's the workforce had risen to over 400 but with the decline of the industry the quarry closed in 1915. The flooded main quarry pit is above the spoil heaps.

The site is well worth visiting as there are some very impressive remains. A pleasant walk following paths starts from the Snowdonia National Park car park in Rhyd Du

A wheel-pit with Rhyd Ddu beyond

goes to and through the quarry. The walk can be continued on to Snowdon Ranger which crosses the Welsh Highland Railway on a couple of occasions.

The Welsh Highland Railway (WHR) or Rheilffordd Eryri is a 25 miles, 40.2 kms long, narrow gauge

The main working area with Rhyd Ddu at upper left and (below) main working area with L to R Moel Hebog, Moel yr Ogof and Moel Lefn forming the skyline

railway with a gauge of 597 mm, 1 foot 11 ½ inches. The railway is part of a 40 miles, 64 kms system that includes the Ffestiniog Railway where it connects at Porthmadog. An unusual fact about the line is that it crosses the standard gauge line there and is the only mixed gauge level crossing in the UK. The first through service from Porthmadog to Caernarfon took place on the 19th February 2011.

The original WHR was formed in 1922 by the merger of two rail companies, the North Wales Narrow Gauge Railways and the Porthmadog, Beddgelert and South Snowdonia Railway which was the later version of the Porthmadog, Croesor and Beddgelert Tram Railway. Back then the service was not successful, its ancient carriages were uncomfortable, the journey too long and, not least, unreliable.

1. *Incline gateway with L to R Mynydd Drws y Coed and Y Garn;*
2. *Walled cutting of incline with Clogwyn Garreg framed by the walls*

Glynrhonwy

Map: Ordnance Survey 1:25,000
Explorer OL 17 Snowdon/Yr Wyddfa.
Grid reference: lower quarry SH 565 607
and the upper quarry SH 560 606

The lower quarry amalgamated many other 18th century 'scratchings'. These were, along with Glynrhonwy upper quarry, Chwarel Bach, Chwarel Fanog, Chwarel Hir, Chwarel Isaf, Fawnog, Cloddfa y Fford, Gloddfa Ganol, Glan y Llyn, Glyn Isaf, Glyn Uchaf, Greaves, Twll Chwil, Twll Glai, Twll Glas, Twll Goch and Wen Fain. Once amalgamated development intensified into one big pit and subsidiary ones. There was a large mill supplied by a locomotive rail system. The quarry was one of the pioneers of internal rail systems.

Being close to Llyn Padarn the quarry was self draining and the ability to dump waste into the lake made this site very efficient. In 1883

Quarry pool of the lower quarry

tonnage produced was 1,789 from 70 men but later on outputs were greater achieving around 40 tons of slate per man per annum. The slate was initially carted to Caernarfon until 1869 then latterly by traction engine.

General view of upper quarry workings and (below) ruined buildings in upper quarry

An incline connection was made to a loading platform on the main line railway (Caernarfon to Llanberis). The quarry closed in 1930.

Between 1940 and 1943 during the Second World War the quarries were requisitioned by the Air Ministry to store over 18,000 tons of bombs and explosives. Subsequently the quarries were used for bomb disposal continuing until 1956 when a building collapsed. It was not until 1975 that the site was cleared and declared safe and free from explosives. The left hand quarry was used as a venue by Ron Howard for the film 'Willow' starring Val Kilmer in 1968.

One of the most dreadful accidents to happen in the area occurred on Wednesday 30th June 1869. It was very hot day. Two carts were carrying nitro-glycerine, to be used in the Glynrhonwy quarries, exploded. Five people and two horses were killed instantly. Another 8 were seriously injured with one of them dying a few days later. The explosion was so fierce that it created two craters 10 feet deep and 30 feet wide! Not a house within a mile radius was left unscathed. No trace of was found of either the horses or two of the men. Some human remains were found a mile away and a wheel from one of the carts was found on the road close to the summit of the road high above!

The upper quarry incorporates Chwarel Fain, Glyn Ganol and Premier Glynrhonwy. Although worked separately both lower and upper quarries became one. The upper quarry developed in the 19th century having two pits in tandem with mills. Again a complex rail system operated here with some cantilevered along rock faces! In 1882 the quarry produced 2,181 tons of slate from a workforce of 90 men. Closure came in 1939 when only 2 men were working.

There is no formal access to these quarries.

1. Entrance to the upper quarry; 2. Degraded incline; 3. Ruined building in upper quarry; 4. The prominent cairn atop a spoil heap with small incline to left

Golwern

Map: Ordnance Survey 1:25,000
Explorer OL 23 Cadair Idris & Llyn Tegid
Grid reference: SH 621 122

Also known as Goleuwern, Golwern Quarry was opened in 1867. By 1872 it was employing 51 men. Slate was brought down the hill on a long incline to the valley road and transported by cart to the ferry at Fairbourne. In the 1890's both Golwern and Henddol quarries operated under one company, Walker and Co. The quarry closed in the late 1920's. HENDDOL QUARRY SH 619 122 is found slightly lower down the hillside and was worked between 1865 and 1871. It was reopened in 1883 producing 401 tons of slate against the 50 tons of Golwern in the same year. Forty men were employed producing 10 tons each and at Golwern 4 men produced around 13 tons per man! When considered with

Stone archway

other slate quarries this was not a great deal. For example the greatest producer of slate, Penrhyn, produced 111,617 tons but with a huge workforce

1. The 'Blue Pool'; 2. Remains of a drum wheel; 3. The fine quarry wall

of 2,838 men who produced around 38 tons each!

The 'Blue Pool' was formed by deliberately filling the quarry pit in 1901 which was to be used as a reservoir for an ambitious scheme to provide Fairbourne with electric lighting. This was undertaken by Arthur McDougal's engineer. Most of the pipes were laid but the scheme folded.

Arthur McDougal became famous through the manufacture of flour and Fairbourne owes its existence to him. He wanted to create an elite resort, South Barmouth, buying the Ynysfaig Estate and surrounding land in 1895, but his plans never materialised and he sold the estate in 1912. Fairbourne, a singularly inappropriate English name, takes its name from the new railway station he built in 1899. His greatest achievement locally perhaps, was the construction of a horse drawn tramway. This was built originally for construction work but extended to the ferry during 1897 and 1898 and used for transporting tourists in the summer. Subsequently the line became the famous narrow gauge railway.

Sadly there is now no access to the Blue Pool due to some people abusing the site as well as leaving lots of litter. There is a circular walk starting from Fairbourne to visit the quarry but before reaching it the walk passes close to Cyfanned Fawr, once an important building dating back to 1748. In the mid 1900s it was the home of Morus Jones a very well known poet and winner of many bardic chairs.

Looking down to Barmouth from Golwern

Hafod y Llan

Map: Ordnance Survey 1:25,000
Explorer OL 17 Snowdon/Yr Wyddfa
Grid reference: SH 613 524

Otherwise known as South Snowdon or Cwm Llan. This quarry is tucked away at the head of Cwm Llan just before the Watkin Path starts its precipitous rise to the summit of Snowdon. The quarry started life in the 1840's. Copper had been mined above the Cwm from 1762 at Braich yr Oen. Although a water wheel powered mill was built at that time plans to build a rail link with Porthmadog came to nought. The finished product was carted out via the cart road serving the copper mine. There was considerable development in the 1860's. The mill was extended and converted to turbine power.

The magnificent incline seen on the first part of the Watkin Path is indeed spectacular. It was built down

View down the Hafod y Llan incline

to Pont Bethania. Output was minimal but Hafod y Llan was the only one to keep its head above water in the Beddgelert area. Sadly the quarry did not recover from the expenditure of the infrastructure

1. The drum house at the top of the Hafod y Llan incline; 2. Part of the Hafod y Llan tramway leading to the top of the incline; 3. The mill area; 4. Barrack ruins

failing to recover from the 1870's slump. The incline ended at Hafod y Llan farm from where slate was carted down Nant Gwynant.

The remains cover quite an extensive area with the mill as the focal point. Close by are the barracks. These paint a forlorn picture and are in a poor state. The tramway leads away from the mill, reached after a short wet section and can be followed all the way to the head of the incline. The view down this is impressive. At the head of the incline is a ruined drum house along with the brakeman's hut. Just before the incline the tramway crosses an earlier one that brought copper down from the Braich yr Oen copper mine. The Braich yr Oen incline in fact has the best stone block sleepers to be found in North Wales. The holes were for the line fixings.

A grand circular walk takes in the Braich yr Oen incline up to the mine before continuing up Yr Aran 747 metres, 2,451 feet. This is followed by a descent to Hafod y Llan slate quarry before continuing down Cwm Llan. Part way down this is Gladstone Rock. On 13th September 1892 William Ewart Gladstone the Prime Minister of Britain for the 4th time delivered a speech from here to 2,000 people to open the Watkin Path. This was named in honour of Sir Edward Watkin a Liberal Member of Parliament and railway entrepreneur. He had retired to a chalet in Cwm Llan. In order for visitors to be able to walk up Snowdon Sir Edward created a path from the already existing one up to the slate quarries to the summit of the mountain. It was the first designated footpath in Britain and the first step towards the opening up of the mountains and countryside for walkers. Gladstone was 83 at the time of his speech!

Cwm Llan was used as the setting for the Khyber Pass in the comedy film 'Carry on up the Khyber'.

Hendre Ddu

Map: Ordnance Survey 1:25,000
Explorer 254 Lleyn Peninsula East/Pen Llŷn
Ardal Ddwyreiniol
Grid reference: SH 517 444

Also known as Prince Llywelyn. First workings here were early in the 19th century but developed further in the 1860's. There was then a steam mill and an incline down to the valley road. Annual tonnage was not high even with 60 men being employed they produced fewer than a 1,000 tons. As a result the enterprise failed. A re-start was made in 1872 again with little success with failure once again in 1880. Another start, made in 1898, also failed.

There are some interesting remains especially at the highest level where there are barracks. These are unusual in that they have very tall windows. Access is up a very rough track from the road going up Cwm Pennant.

1. *Plas Hendre; 2. A typical 'shot hole'*

The ruins of the barrack

Moelfre

Map: Ordnance Survey 1:25,000
Explorer OL 254 Lleyn Peninsula East/Pen
Llŷn Ardal Ddwyreiniol
Grid reference: SH 521 451

Another quarry developed in Cwm Pennant in the 1860's was on the site of earlier 'scratchings'. Copper was also trialled but with little success. That was left to Cwm Ciprwth, further up the valley, to exploit that resource. It was a difficult site to work. Slate from the quarry was taken out via a cutting then a tunnel before being up-hauled to the mill. The finished product was then transported down to the valley by an incline, part of which is walked up when visiting the site. Because of the cost of transporting the slate the working closed but re-opened again in the early 1870's. A new, lower tunnel gave access to a new incline down to a valley floor mill. The quarry employed

Wheel pit close to start of the track up to the main quarry workings

some 30 men who produced 600 tons per annum. It closed in 1880 but sporadic working continued up to the 1930's.

It is an interesting site to visit as there are several levels to explore

Mid-level ruins

with some ruins. At valley level are launder pillars and a wheel pit. On the walk up to the quarry an old incline goes up past a ruined drum house to reach the spoil heaps and levels on the left with the impressive quarry on the right. There is another quarry on the left when the path levels. Above this is a fine circular powder house.

Launder pillar above the wheel pit close to start of the track up to the main quarry workings

1. *The ruined powder house above Moelfre Quarry; 2. Dressing shed*

Moelwyn

Map: Ordnance Survey 1:25,000
Explorer OL 18 Harlech, Porthmadog &
Bala/Y Bala
Grid reference: SH 661 442

Includes Bwlch Stwlan SH 656 442 and 658 442 and Cloddfa Sion Llwyd SH 661 439. Initial prospecting as to the possibility of extracting slate commenced in the 1820's and again in the 1840's but it was 1860 before a company was formed. It was never very profitable. Other entrepreneurs took up the challenge but none prospered. Inevitably the mine finally closed in 1897. Moelwyn was a largely underground producer set in superb and dramatic surroundings at an altitude of 520 metres, 1,706 feet. A mill was constructed some 70 metres, 230 feet lower than the workings below Llyn Stwlan and had 6 saw benches and 7 dressing machines. These were driven by a 12 metres x 1.2

Moelwyn Mine and spoil heap below Craigysgafn

metres, 40 feet x 4 feet waterwheel with water from Llyn Stwlan.

Barracks and family houses were constructed at the site. The children went to school in Tanygrisiau. The mine was producing slate in the 1870's and again in the 1890's but closure came in 1900. Initially transportation was by packhorse down Cwm Maesgwm on a track built in 1826. Since 1860 they used the Ffestiniog Railway having used the spectacular inclines.

Many traces of the lower infrastructure such as inclines and mill area were lost when the reservoir was built. Access is by walking up the tarmac access to Llyn Stwlan and walking clockwise around it to the ruins and workings.

1. Powder house ruin below Craigysgafn; 2. Part of the old tramway; 3. Llyn Stwlan below Moelwyn Bach on the left and Craigysgafn on the right showing the inclines

Nantlle Vale/Tŷ Mawr

Map: Ordnance Survey 1:25,000 Explorer OL 254 Lleyn Peninsula East/Pen Llyn Ardal Ddwyreiniol
Grid reference: SH 497 524

Also known as Tŷ Mawr East. It opened in the 1860's as a part of the original Tŷ Mawr workings. It was one of the largest concerns on the southern side of Dyffryn Nantlle. Production was never high. In 1882 only 150 tons were realised from 20 men! It closed around 1910.

I have included this purely on the basis of the engine house chimney, a fine feature, close to the B4418.

Snowdon from close to Nantlle Vale/ Tŷ Mawr with Llyn Nantlle Uchaf in the foreground

Tŷ Mawr boiler house chimney

Nant y Fron

*Map: Ordnance Survey 1:25,000
Explorer OL 254 Lleyn Peninsula East/Pen
Llŷn Ardal Ddwyreiniol
Grid reference: SH 486 518*

A chaos of ruination at Nant y Fron

Other names are Eryri and Fronheulog These incorporated New Fronlog and Upper Tyddyn Agnes. Work commenced in 1840 with tandem pits followed by a third. This though was below the mill. As such a double acting water balance incline was probably used. The quarry operated intermittently with a reportedly highest output of 2,000 tons per annum. However, in 1862 the reported tonnage was 1,862. A maximum of 90 men were employed. A waterwheel originally powered the mill and two water wheel hauled inclines. The quarry was connected to the Caernarvonshire Slate Quarries Railway and operated in conjunction with FRONLOG SH 489 517. In 1882 Fronlog became part of Nant y Fron having produced some 1,642 tons from 98 men in that year. Nant y Fron closed in 1939 but small scale working commenced again in the 1970's and 1980's. The slate here has a rich green colour.

There is much to see here and is well worth visiting.

Looking across to the huge spoil heap of Cilgwyn. Talysarn village is on the left and (below) ruins of the mill area with Mynydd Mawr to the right of Moel Eilio.

Pen y Bryn/Gallt y Fedw

Map: Ordnance Survey 1:25,000
Explorer OL
Grid reference Pen y Bryn: SH 505 538
Gallt y Fedw: SH 499 535

This incorporates Cae Cilgwyn and includes Herbert's Quarry & Twll Penybryn, Cloddfa Lon, Dew's Quarry, Hen Dwll, Twll Balast & Twll Mawr, David's Quarry, Middle Quarry, New Pen y Bryn, Owen's Quarry and Twll Ismaliod. This was one of the earliest slate quarries to open in Snowdonia opening in 1770. By 1882 it employed 240 men who produced 5,083 tons of slate a respectable 21 tons per man. There were 4 pits next to the mill area. Initially two waterwheels supplied the power. Later steam was used for both pumping and winding. The quarry was a pioneer and instigator of chain inclines in 1830.

Blondins supplemented these and

1. *The winding engine house chimney;*
2. *Twll Mawr; 3. The entry track into the derelict buildings at Gallt y Fedw*

continued being used until the late 1930's. One of the inclines went down to the Nantlle Railway. This terminated here before being extended to Pen yr Orsedd. The quarry was taken over by the nearby

Dorothea in 1836. Pen y Bryn closed in the late 1890's but small scale working continued until the 1940's but after the Second World War the owners of Dorothea unsuccessfully tried to re-open it by making road access.

The majority of the remains are found on the northerly and newer mills section with the walls of the quite large mill still standing as do the barracks and fine chimney of a winding engine house.

Nearby and associated with Pen y Bryn is the cluttered site of GALLT Y FEDW. It was otherwise known as Alexandria, Victoria, Y Foel, and incorporated Cae Ysgybor, Twll Mug, Old Pen y Bryn. Commencing in the mid 19th century these were open pit workings that were amalgamated from ancient 'scratchings'. Steam operated inclines took material to a six saw-table mill. The finished product went out via the incline which firstly crossed the Nantlle Railway before joining it. Output was small with only a few hundred tons per annum from around a dozen men. Working persevered until the 1930's. One of the most striking remains here is the roof of a ruin that has coloured slates, a feature of the area. Incline formations remain. Another feature is an impressive length of a retaining wall.

1. Some of the ruined quarry buildings;
2. The winding engine house chimney and walls of the mill; 3. Ruins at Gallt y Fedw; 4. Old steps on the side of a building at Gallt y Fedw; 5. A decayed incline; 6. Cluttered building ruins at Gallt y Fedw; 7. The neglected patterned roof of a ruined building in Gallt y Fedw; 8. Ruin below the spoil heap of Cilgwyn and the access road; 9. Launder pillars at Gallt y Fedw

Ratgoed

Map: Ordnance Survey 1:25,000
Explorer OL 23 Cadair Idris & Llyn Tegid
Grid reference: SH 787 119

Part of the Ratgoed tramway

Also known as Alltgoed or Ralltgoed. Slate was extracted, in the main, from underground working. The early work was undertaken close to the valley floor on what is known as the Broad Vein. Extraction of the main Narrow Vein slate were on 6 levels high up on the side of Mynydd Cymerau. The annual output peaked at around 800 tons. However, the usual annual tonnage was nearer 434 as recorded in 1882 from a workforce of 35 men. The mine produced mainly slab with some being finished work as in mantelpieces.

Having closed in the late 1840's it re-opened in 1851 and expanded. It was run by John Rowlands under the title of Alltgoed Consols. This was a partnership that also owned Gaewern and Braich Goch. Rowlands was sacked due to shareholder discontent in the 1860's. The original owner Horatio Nelson Hughes took back control. Transporting the slate was eased greatly when the 2′ 3″, 686 millimetres Ratgoed tramway started operating after the opening of the Corris Railway. Expansion grew as a result of this and continued to run profitably through 1878. As slate prices dropped throughout the whole slate industry small operations such as Ratgoed suffered. Production still continued in the 1880's but with reduced output. By the 1890's it became more profitable but by the end of the century accessible material for roofing slate was running dry. The then owner tried to sell the business in 1897. By 1900 the workforce had been dismissed.

Briefly re-opening in 1901 it closed again in 1903 as the price for slab fell. In 1907 there was another re-start. By the end of 1911 there were more than 30 men working. The First World war brought difficulties and by 1918 only 6 men were working. After the war ended the struggle to extract slate continued. In 1924 a local company Hall, Harber & Thomas Ltd. purchased Ratgoed. They also owned the Llwyngwern quarry about 5 miles, 8 kms, to the south, now the site for the Centre of Alternative Technology

1. 'Cadbury House';
2. The Blacksmith's workshop

CAT. The workforce then doubled but declined steadily through the late 1920s. The quarry struggled on through the 1930's and during World

War II but the inevitable closure came in 1946.

The Nant Ceiswyn flows through Cwm Ratgoed On the left before reaching the valley workings is a white house known as 'Cadbury House'. It was bought by the Cadbury chocolate family in the 1960's. The family were, for the time, kind to their staff allowing them to use the house for holidays. It was also used by the Bourneville family who used it as a base for hill walking. Supposedly there is a well hereabouts also called Ffynnon Badarn, St. Padarn's Well.

The fine ruin with an arched doorway and windows was the Calvinistic Methodist chapel which opened in 1871. Past this is another ruin, the blacksmith's. Behind it are the ruins of the slate dressing sheds. To the right are more ruins with the one closest to the track, the weigh bridge. Up to the right is an overgrown incline. A walled section of old tramway leads to Ratgoed Hall on the left. This was owned by the quarry owner Horatio Nelson Hughes, a wealthy Liverpudlian. He built the Hall in 1870. In 1940 it became a Youth Hostel. Passing this through the old metal gate open country continues to Dolgoed an old Quaker House. This is possibly the oldest house in Meirionnydd and has been in the hands of the same family since the 1600's.

To the left and slightly above is Ceiswyn Farmhouse. This was built in the 1500's. The Red Brigands of Dinas Mawddwy were an infamous group of brigands, or highwaymen, with predominantly red hair. They were a lawless group and one of their attacks achieving notoriety occurred here. They captured and killed a local judge, Sir Lewis Owain, in a revenge attack for having sentenced some of their group tried and executed. The judge's companion was Sion Lloyd who survived the ambush. Legend tells us that Lloyd hid swords in the chimney in case of another attack!

Rhos

Map: Ordnance Survey 1:25,000 Explorer OL 17 Snowdon/Yr Wyddfa.
Grid reference: SH 729 564

Also known as Capel Curig or Rhos y Goelcerth. This was large pit working and made extensive use of water power. It initially opened in the early 1850's. At first slate was brought out through a short tunnel, later becoming a cutting, by tram to the mill. As the quarry deepened a water-powered up haulage system was used. A 9 metres, 30 feet waterwheel used for this purpose could also have pumped water out of the pit. At the mill there was a waterwheel 5.5 metres, 18 feet. Later a drainage tunnel was cut which enabled the use of a water balance as well as providing for the easy removal of spoil.

In 1935 the water balance was replaced with a chain incline again powered by a water wheel. The mill

1. The main mill area with Moel Siabod behind; 2. The barracks at the entrance to the quarry

was the last plant to be worked by water wheel and was of impressive size. It had 22 Greaves saws, a planer

*The barracks at the entrance to the quarry and (below)
Launder pillars with Moel Siabod on the skyline*

and some mechanical dressers in the *waliau*. Output in 1882 was 1,285 tons from 45 men. In 1937-8 the number of men employed was 52. Final closure came in 1952 with half the number of men from the pre-war days.

Access is difficult but can be achieved although care is needed. The land is private and is outside recognised access land although the ruined barracks have often been photographed. It is an exposed but a very interesting site to visit.

1. *The mill area;*
2. *The decaying mill ruins*

Talysarn

Map: Ordnance Survey 1:25,000 Explorer OL 17 Snowdon/Yr Wyddfa.
Grid reference: SH 495 535

Little remains of Talysarn other than its fine flooded pit. It incorporated some 12 other minor workings. These were Carnarvon and Bangor and Twll Mawr. Incorporated too were Allt Llevhi, Blaen Cae, Cloddfa Fawr, Cloddfa'r Onnen Fach, Cloddfa'r Onnen Fawr, Chwarel Coch, Talysarn Bach, Twll Penditch, Twll Penuparc and Twll Ffactri. There were possibly more that were merely just surface 'scratchings'. Production started in 1790. By 1829 there was a water balance. A Rag and Chain pump was also operational. These were constructed to pump the pits and were basically tubes through which an endless chain ran with small buckets attached. A windlass was turned on the surface and the water that was

Arch at Talysarn Hall

collected dumped into a tank when buckets reached the top. A basic rag and chain pump could deliver around 12 gallons a minute.

In its heyday Talysarn was the fourth largest in Dyffryn Nantlle with production culminating in 1882 at

The flooded quarry pit and (below) Tal-y-sarn village

8,210 tons. Around 400 men worked there at the time. The other minor workings were used as convenient tips for the waste material. An incline connected the workings to the Nantlle Railway. Closure came in 1946.

Talysarn village was once a hive of industry. Nowadays it is a peaceful little place. Two famous people lived there, Robert Williams Parry 1884–1956 an influential Welsh poet and the Reverend John Jones 1796–1857 one of the most influential Methodists of his age. The main railway line reached Talysarn in 1872 although the quarry itself was connected by an incline to the horse drawn Nantlle Railway.

Plas Talysarn was the home of the Robinson family, the owners of Talysarn Quarry. This was once a very grand building along with its outbuildings but today sadly, it is in a very bad state of dereliction and decay with no access as much of it is now fenced off.

Close by was CLODDFA'R COED quarry. At one time it was one of the four largest quarries in the valley. The others being CILGWYN SH 501 540, Talysarn itself and PEN Y BRYN (see chapter on this). Cilgwyn is now totally obliterated having been used as a council tip! It is thought that slate quarrying commenced at Cilgwyn in the 13th century. However, none of them could outstrip the growth of DOROTHEA SH 500 532 or PEN YR ORSEDD SH 509 539. (Both these are described in Vol 1). Notably the pumping waterwheel was replaced by a steam engine in 1807. Unfortunately due to bad judgement and careless excavation it fell into the pit in 1817! Due to the success of Cloddfa'r Coed between 1850 and 1870 the village of Talysarn developed quickly. The quarry operated on an intermittent basis until the Second World War, doing especially well in the 1890's but pathetic tonnages were the norm. For example in 1873 4 men only produced 8 tons. Ten men worked there in 1938 and was connected to the Nantlle

Railway. The whole site has now been landscaped and nothing remains to be seen.

Access is via the rough public path/track from either Nantlle or Talysarn and passes the 152 metres, 500 feet deep flooded pit of Dorothea quarry. There is free car parking at either end.

1. One of many ruined buildings; 2. Ruins close to Talysarn Hall; 3. Steps leading up into an office

NATIONAL SLATE MUSEUM

Situated on the outskirts of Llanberis close to Llyn Padarn this tells the story about a way of life. Not only is it the best place for experiencing life as it was during the slate mining days it also gives an insight into the rigours of extracting and fashioning the slate. There are regular demonstrations on how slates are split. There is operational machinery and the 15.4 metres high water wheel is the largest on the British mainland. The experience is free other than the Council operated car park. A whole day could be spent here looking at the exhibits and exploring one or more of the slate paths described earlier. For more information look at the web site: www.slate@museumwales.ac.uk or telephone 0300 1112333

NOTE when visiting the following show mines please be aware that the temperature inside is well below that outside in summer. It is between 8 to 10 degrees C (around 50 degrees F). As such it is advisable to wear warm clothing. Wear shoes or boots having a good grip as floors can be slippery.

LLECHWEDD SLATE CAVERNS

This is situated on the outskirts of Blaenau Ffestiniog some ¾ mile north of the town. There are many attractions here not least is the story of the Llechwedd Caverns in the interpretive centre. This also shows how slate was extracted and processed. There is also a reconstructed village showing how the miners lived. Access to the underground workings is by a funicular railway. Descending over 500 feet it is the steepest passenger railway in Britain. The tour involves visiting 10 huge chambers and ½ mile of tunnels to arrive at a very beautiful underground lake. In fact the mine has over 25 miles of tunnels. Other attractions here include mountain biking, zip lines and a huge underground trampoline. For more information look at the web site: www.llechwedd-slate-caverns.co.uk or telephone 01766 830306.

Llechwedd was first mined in 1848 and slate production was greatly improved by new technologies such as slate cutting saws in 1851. In the 1920's electricity was introduced which powered the underground railway systems. John Greaves was the owner of Llechwedd as well as several others in the area and he was much involved with the Ffestiniog Railway. This enabled slate products being transported to a private quay in Porthmadog before being shipped to the four corners of the world. Germany had a great demand for Llechwedd slate products.

There are other developments here – Bounce Below, Zip World Titan and Antur Stiniog. This last is a not for profit organisation set up in 2007 with a view 'to develop the potential of the Outdoor Sector in the Ffestiniog area in a sustainable and innovative way for the benefit of the local residents and economy'. They have developed a series of exciting mountain bike trails in the area and are aiming to develop the disused railway line between Blaenau Ffestiniog and Trawsfynydd. A unique, to the UK, Velorail project is also planned along this. The concept uses low carbon, sustainable bicycle technology to propel an adapted carriage along the disused railway line. This would make it attractive to families.

LLANFAIR SLATE CAVERNS

Although smaller than Llechwedd Caverns it is no less impressive. Situated not far from Harlech on the A496 coast road the mine is entered down Jacobs Ladder and you are free to explore. On emerging there is a breath-taking view of Cardigan Bay, stretching all the way from the Preseli Mountains in Carmarthenshire to the Llyn Peninsula, whilst closer to is Shell Island. For more information look at the web site: www.llanfairs-latecaverns.co.uk or telephone 01766 780247.

Slate was mined here between 1890 and 1910. Here there it is possible to explore the caverns by yourself. Some of the scenes of the 1995 film 'First Knight' were filmed here.

KING ARTHUR'S LABYRINTH

A part of Corris Craft Centre, close to Machynlleth, this show mine is explored by boat and foot. Themed on King Arthur it is best described as an underground storytelling adventure. A mysterious hooded boatman takes you through a magical waterfall into the world of King Arthur and the Dark Ages. Once the boat is docked the 'hooded' boatman guides you through vast caverns and tunnels telling stories about those times as well as some Welsh legends. Light and sound bring these to life. The Labyrinth is part of the Braich Goch Mine and is on level 6. For more information look at the web site www.kingarthurslabyrinth.co.uk or telephone 01654 761584. Note that during winter months staff are often not present so delays in returning calls may be experienced.

Next to the Labyrinth there is a Stone Circle. A twisting path in the simple maze hides 8 mythical stories with some very interesting characters. Find all the clues and you win a prize!

CORRIS MINE EXPLORERS

For the adventurous Corris Mine Explorers gives people a chance to explore the ancient working of Braich Goch Mine. Although there are 7 levels the exploration covers 3 of these, levels 4, 5 and 6. There are three trips available: Taster, a 2 hour Mine Explorer and a ½ day (4 hours) Mine Expedition. Further information and bookings can be made at www.corrismineexplorers.co.uk or telephone 01654 761244.

Slate quarrying at Corris dates back to the 14th century when the Foel Grochan quarry above Aberllefenni was first mined The Braich Goch and Gaewern mines began around 1812 with Gaewern being the first of the two to be worked with Braich Goch itself starting in 1836. In 1848 working at Gaewern ceased and re-started in 1853. During its heyday some 250 men worked in the mine in 1878 and around 7,000 tons of slab and roofing slates were mined. Rising costs and demand saw the mine company collapse in 1906 although 6 companies continued work until 1970 when the mine finally closed.

ELECTRIC MOUNTAIN

Visiting the vast underground tunnels and chambers of this underground power station is an amazing experience. But why build one here? In the 1950's a pumped storage scheme was undertaken at Blaenau Ffestiniog and was highly successful. As such another scheme was planned. The ideal situation was found on Elidir Fawr. Marchlyn Mawr a small lake below the summit and in the valley Llyn Peris. The huge rambling scar of the Dinorwig quarries provided the ideal place in which to build tunnels to house the power station It took 10 years to build as well as enlarging the lakes and was opened by Prince Charles in 1984. Further information can be obtained at www.electricmountain.co.uk or telephone 01286 870636.

Quarrying first took place in 1787. Production increased after 1824 to the extent that around 100,000 tons of slate was produced. Bear in mind that for every 10 tons of rock quarried only 1 ton was usable! At its peak in the late 19th century over 3,000 men worked there and at the time it was the largest opencast slate producer in the country. By 1930 the workforce had shrunk to 2,000 and in 1969 production ceased. The slate vein is almost vertical. As such it was worked in stepped galleries.

INIGO JONES SLATE WORKS

Initially the works were established in 1861 to prefabricate school writing slates. Nowadays, self-guided tours of the works give an opportunity to have a go at calligraphy and engraving a piece of slate that you get to keep as a souvenir. There is a large showroom where its slate products are available for purchase as are other Welsh and Celtic gifts. Tours were introduced in the early 1980's by popular demand and commences with a video presentation followed by wandering through the workshops accompanied with a personal taped commentary. There is also a café opening at 10.00 to 17.00. The site is open every day of the year excepting for Christmas and Boxing Days and New Year's Day from 09.00 to 17.00 with a last tour at 16.00. Dogs are welcome. More information can be obtained at www.inigojones.co.uk or calling 01286 830242.

ZIP WORLD

Opening in March 2013 ZIP WORLD VELOCITY in Bethesda quickly achieved international fame. There is a pair of zip lines each a mile long where it is possible to achieve speeds of 100 mph! The wires are 500 feet above the ground making the experience the nearest thing to human flight. The Adventure Terminal provides stunning views of Velocity, Penrhyn Quarry and the lake. Further information can be obtained at www.zipworld.co.uk or telephone 01248 601444.

GO BELOW

For some great underground adventures and challenges this company has a big selection of trips from 5 hours to all day. The mines they explore are some of the longest and deepest in Snowdonia. Mines such as Cwmorthin above Tanygrisiau and Rhiwbach in Cwm Penmachno have a variety of trips. They have bases in Tanygrisiau close to Blaenau Ffestiniog and at Conwy Falls near to Betws y Coed. Further information and bookings can be made at www.go-below.co.uk or telephone 01690 710108.

CENTRE FOR ALTERNATIVE TECHNOLOGY (CAT)

This is situated in the old quarry of Llyngwern just off the A487 some 3 miles north of Machynlleth. There is much to discover here regarding living a greener life form what can be done to your home, how Britain can become Zero Carbon, Green Bookshop, the water balance cliff railway, information on renewable energy, mole hole and quarry trail. There is also a café.

Further information can be found at www.cat.org.uk or telephone 01654 705950 or email visit@cat.org.uk.

Slate Heritage Narrow Gauge Railways

These modern day tourist trains had a much darker beginning as they were primarily used for transporting slate from quarry to port. Six of these are within easy reach of the mines and quarries described herein.

FFESTINIOG RAILWAY

The Ffestiniog Railway is located mainly in the National Park. Starting in Porthmadog the delightful and scenic 13½ mile, 21.6 kilometres journey ends at Blaenau Ffestiniog, once the heart of the slate industry.
www.festrail.co.uk

WELSH HIGHLAND RAILWAY

The longest heritage railway in the UK. It travels 25 miles, 40 kilometres from Porthmadog to Caernarfon. The scenery is superb all the way for the 2¼ hour journey.
www.festrail.co.uk

LLANBERIS LAKE RAILWAY

Starting in Llanberis the 5 mile, 8 kms return journey ends at the far end of Llyn Padarn. Originally it went through to Caernarfon and transported slate from Dinorwig and Vivian quarries to Port Dinorwic.
www.lake-railway.co.uk

CORRIS RAILWAY

This very important railway was used to transport slate from the mines around Corris. A short section of the line has been resurrected and is now established as one of the 'Great Little Railways of Wales'.
www.corris.co.uk

TALYLLYN RAILWAY

This 14½ mile, 23 kms return journey commences in Tywyn to terminate at Nant Gwernol. The line was constructed to transport slate from Bryn Eglwys quarry.
www.talyllyn.co.uk

FAIRBOURNE MINIATURE RAILWAY

The 2 mile, 3.2 kms journey from Fairbourne ends at a summer only ferry at its terminus on the Mawddach Estuary where a ferry can be taken to Barmouth.
www.office@fairbournerailway.com

Some Slate Mining and Quarrying Terminology

Adit: The entrance to a mine tunnel from the surface

Balanced incline: An incline with two railway tracks where the descent of the loaded wagons brought up the empty ones

Barracks: The accommodation area used by quarrymen usually through the week but occasionally all year

Black Powder: The original explosive used prior to dynamite

Block: A large piece of quarried slate

Blondin: A wire rope, supported by wooden or iron towers, where a system of pulleys would raise, move and lower rock

Caban: A small shelter built from the waste rock by the miners normally used as a place of rest and at lunchtimes

Chain incline: A suspended incline using a wire rope instead of a railway line and inclined plane

Chamber: An underground working area that is up to 70 feet wide

Chwarel: The Welsh name for quarry

Cowjian: A plug chisel that is used for splitting blocks

Cup-boarding: This is the very dangerous practise of cutting into roofing pillars in order to get cheap or free slate

Cyfell: A long wide knife used to trim roofing slates to size

Drum: A horizontal drum around which the wire rope of a balanced incline was wound. Often made from wood

Fire-setting: A very old mining method used to weaken the slate by building a fire against a working face and then quenching with water. Going back almost 2,000 years it was described by Pliny the Elder in 77 AD

Floor: The working level of a quarry or mine and usually numbered

Jwmpah: A long weighted rod weighted close to an end used for manually boring a holeLong weighted rod used to manually bore a hole. Used before the advent of compressed air drills

Launder: A trough used for conveying water to a water wheel

Leat: An artificial watercourse or aqueduct dug into the ground, especially one supplying water to a mill

Level: Horizontal tunnel driven for access or drainage

Mill: The building where slate is reduced by using machinery. At first water was used then latterly by electricity

Mine: An underground excavation made to extract the slate. Quarry, pit and opencast are used for workings open to daylight

Pillar: A column of slate left to support the roof above

Pillar robbing: Same as cup-boarding

Plug and feathers: A tool that consisted of two half round, tapered, short bars and a wedge. The two bars are inserted into a pre-drilled hole and then the wedge is hammered down between them, splitting the rock. Along with fire-setting, this was a common method of level driving before the introduction of gunpowder

Pric Mesur: A serrated stick with nail in the end that was used to mark out roofing slate sizes

Quarry: The distinction, in law, between a quarry and mine is somewhat unclear. The term quarry implies that the workings are open to the sky

Revetment: A term used for a retaining wall

Rhys: A large mallet used to break up large slate blocks

Rubbish: The waste rock from the mining or quarrying process. It took around 10 tons of rock to produce 1 ton of usable slate

Shot hole: The hole bored into the slate for the insertion of gunpowder

Strike: A tunnel bored horizontally into the slate vein

Terrace: A working level of an open quarry. These, like levels, were numbered

Un-topping: The term used for removing the earth and rock from above the underground workings to remove pillars to gain cheap slate

Twll: A surface pit working

Waliau: Open fronted sheds where slate was hand trimmed and dressed

Water balance: A type of incline where the weight of water was used to raise wagons

Winding or Drum House: This was built to support the winding mechanism at the head of an incline

A Selection of Further Reading

Snowdonia Slate – The story with photographs by Des Marshall
ISBN 978-1-84524-291-6

Exploring Snowdonia's Slate Heritage – 26 great walks by Des Marshall
ISBN 978-1-908748-52-2

Day Walks from the Slate Trail by Des Marshall
ISBN 978-1-84524-290-9

Snowdonia Slate Trail by Aled Owen
ISBN 978-1-898481-80-5

Gazetteer of Slate Quarrying in Wales by Alun John Richards
ISBN 1-84524-074-X

The Slate Railways of Wales by Alun John Richards
ISBN 0-86381-689-4

Welsh Slate Craft by Alun John Richards
ISBN 1-84527-029-0

Slate Quarrying in Corris by Alun John Richards
ISBN 1-84524-068-5

Slate Quarrying in Wales by Alun John Richards
ISBN 1-84527-026-6

Cwm Gwyfrai by Gwynfor Pierce Jones and Alun John Richards
ISBN 0-86381-897-8

Welsh Slate by David Gwyn
ISBN 978-1-871184-51-8

Within these Hills – A study of Corris Uchaf by Sara Eade
ISBN 978-0-9565652-1-1

The North Wales Quarrymen 1874–1922 by R. Merfyn Jones
ISBN 978-1-78316-175-1

COMPACT CYMRU

COMPACT CYMRU
– MORE SNOWDONIA TITLES:

www.carreg-gwalch.cymru

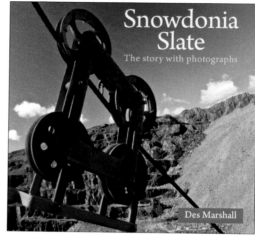

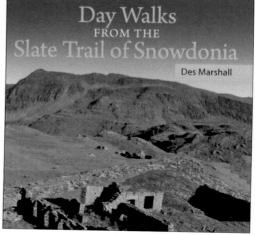